I CAN READ IT ALL BY MYSELF · Beginner Books

To Nancy
7th Birthday
Nov 30 1980

The Beginner Book of
THINGS TO MAKE

FUN STUFF YOU CAN MAKE
ALL BY YOURSELF

By
ROBERT LOPSHIRE

Formerly published as HOW TO MAKE FLIBBERS, ETC.

BEGINNER BOOKS A Division of Random House, Inc.

To my four favorite Flibber Makers,
Martin, Howard, Terry and Vicky.

The Beginner Book of
THINGS TO MAKE

How to Make
a
Zum Zum Fiddle

1 – Get a big
cardboard box.
Get some
strong string.

2 – Make a hole in the
bottom of the box.

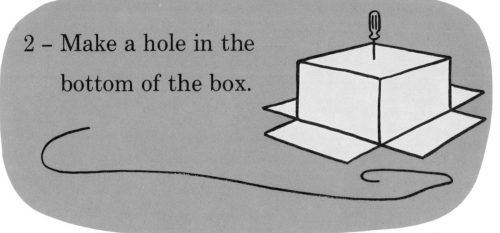

3 – Tie a little stick
on the end of the string.
Pull the string through
the hole in the box.

5 – Tie the string
to a broom.

6 – Hold the broom
like this . . .

. . . and make crazy music!

How to Make
Limp Lamps

1 – Get a piece of paper
   and some scissors.

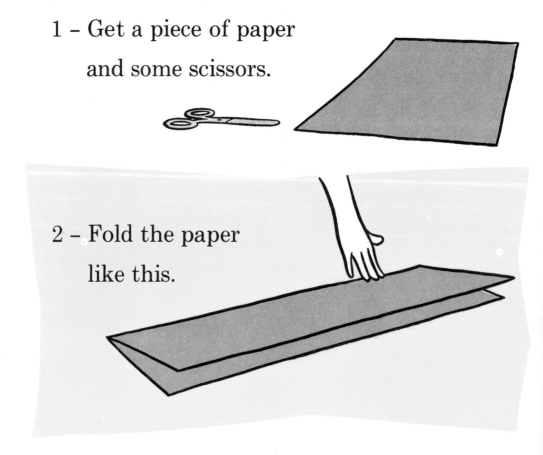

2 – Fold the paper
   like this.

3 – Now cut the paper
   like this.

4 – Unfold the paper.
   Bend it around
   like this.
   Stick the two
   ends together.

5 – Cut another piece
   of paper. Stick it
   on for a handle.

Make a lot of Limp Lamps.
Hang them up. Have a party!

How to Make

a

Humdinger

1 – Get a button . . .

a very big one.

2 – Find a piece of string.

3 – Put the string
in the button
like this.

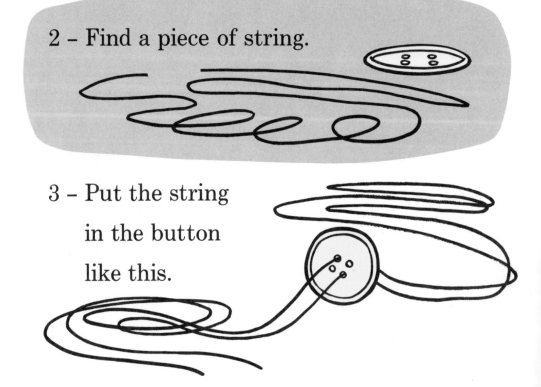

4 – Tie a knot
in the string.

5 – Hold the string
and twirl it.
Wind it up.

6 – Then pull and let go.
Pull HARD! And let go.

Keep it going.
It may go FOREVER!

7

How to Make

a

Flibber

1 – Get a newspaper.

Get an old one.

2 – Put three pieces

on the floor like this.

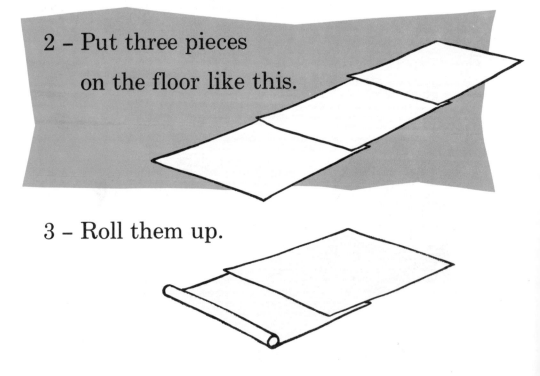

3 – Roll them up.

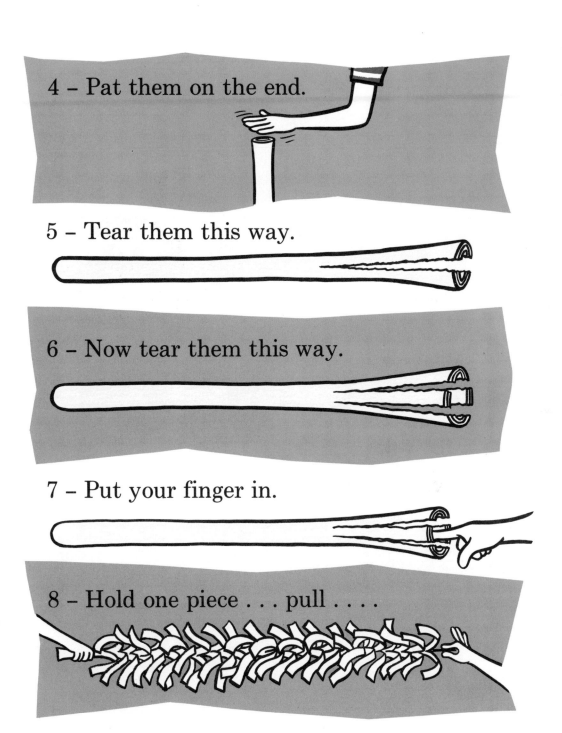

4 – Pat them on the end.

5 – Tear them this way.

6 – Now tear them this way.

7 – Put your finger in.

8 – Hold one piece . . . pull . . . .

And, now you have a Flibber!

How to Make

a

Sweet Pete

1 – Ask your mother
   for an orange,
   a toothpick,
   and some cloves.

2 – Take the toothpick.
   Make small holes
   in the orange
   for Pete's eyes, nose
   and mouth.

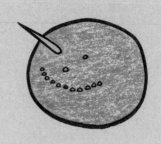

3 – Stick cloves

in the holes.

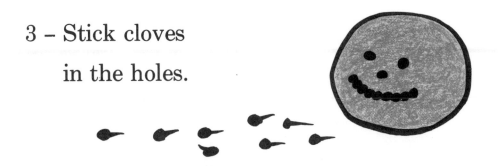

4 – Now make holes

for his hair.

Make a lot of them.

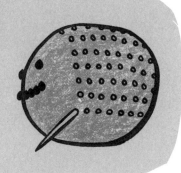

5 – Stick more cloves

in those holes.

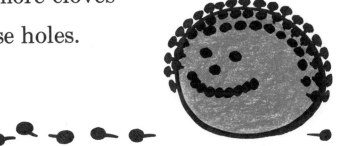

Keep Pete in your room.

He will make it smell fine!

How to Make

a

Whirligig

1 – Get a piece of paper.
   Get a bead, a pin,
   and a stick.

2 – Cut the paper
   four times
   like this.

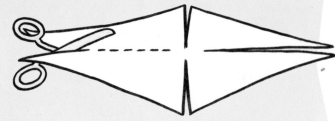

3 – Pull four pieces
   of the paper over
   like this.

4 – Put the pin through
   the paper like this.

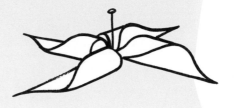

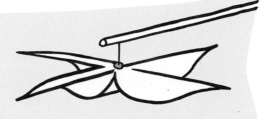

5 – Put the bead on the pin.

6 – Push the pin
   into the stick.

7 – Now go out and run.
   Make your Whirligig whirl!

How to Make
Party Mats

1 – All you need are
scissors and
two pieces
of colored paper.

2 – Fold, and cut
one piece
like this.

3 – Cut the other
   piece into strips.

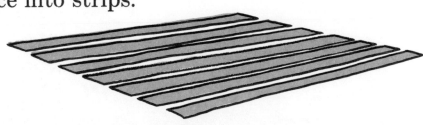

4 – Lay the first
   piece down flat.
   Take a strip and
   go over and under
   like this.

5 – Do this with
   all the strips.

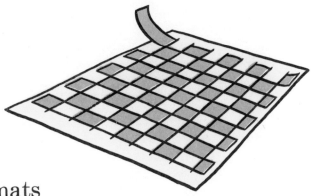

6 – Make a lot of mats
   and have a party.

How to Grow

a

Jungle

1 – Ask your mother

for a sweet potato.

2 – Get four toothpicks

and a glass of water.

16

3 – Put the toothpicks
in the potato
like this.

4 – Put the potato in
the water like this.

5 – Keep it wet,
and your Jungle
will grow.

But be careful!
Look out for those tigers!

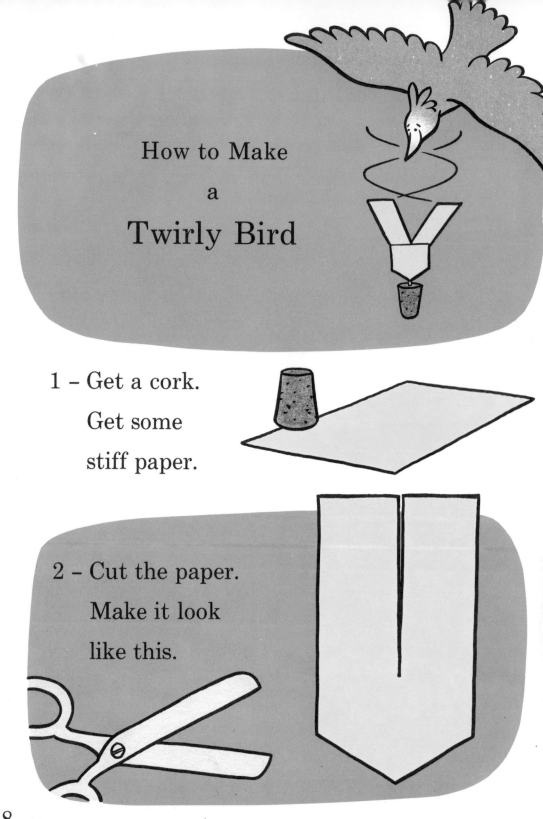

How to Make

a

Twirly Bird

1 – Get a cork.
Get some
stiff paper.

2 – Cut the paper.
Make it look
like this.

18

3 – Bend the paper
   like this.

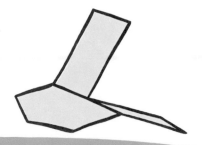

4 – Stick a toothpick
   on the paper
   with stickum.

5 – Now push
   the toothpick
   into the cork.

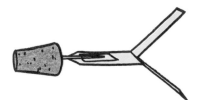

6 – Take your bird outside
   and throw him in the air.

How to Make

a

Screecher

1 – Get some
paper.

2 – Cut a piece
of paper this big.

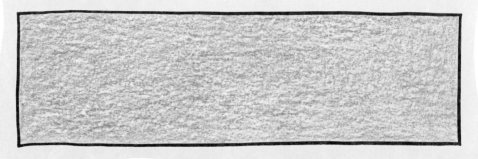

3 – Fold the paper
and cut it
like this.

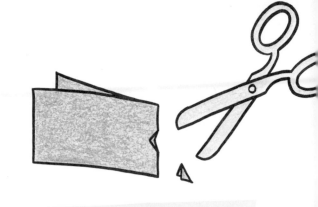

4 – Fold it again.
Make it look
like this.

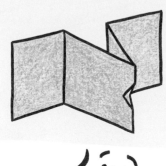

5 – Hold it up to
your mouth
this way.

6 – Now blow!
Blow hard!

You can call your friends
this way . . . .

21

How to Make

a

Yakky Pup

1 – Get a paper bag.

Not too big.

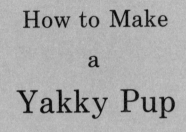

2 – Get some crayons, too.

3 – Draw a face like this.

4 – Draw the mouth here.

5 – Cut some ears out of paper.

6 – Color the ears
and stick them on.

7 – Put your hand
in the bag.
Move your fingers
and make him talk.

He will talk with you for hours!

How to Make
Potato Prints

1 – Ask your mother
for a potato, a dish,
some paper,
and paint.

2 – Ask her to cut
the potato in half.

3 – Have her cut
   one half so it
   looks like this.

4 – Put some paint
   on the dish.
   Dip the potato
   in the paint.

5 – Now press the potato
   down on the paper.
   Do this all over
   the paper.

What do you do with it now?
Turn the page and see . . . .

How to Make

a

Present for Dad

1 – Take your Potato Print
   and a can
   like this one.

2 – Cut the paper.
   Cut off a piece
   as wide as the can.

3 – Stick the paper
around the can.

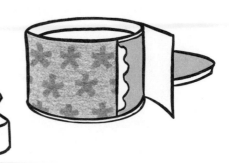

4 – Put the top
of the can
on the other piece.
Draw around it.

5 – Now cut it out.

6 – Stick it on the can top.

Your dad will keep his money
and buttons and stuff in it.

How to Make
a
Phony Phone

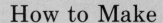

1 – Get two paper cups . . .

2 – . . . and a long piece of thread.

3 – Make a hole in each cup,

a very small pinhole.

4 – Pull the thread
through the holes.

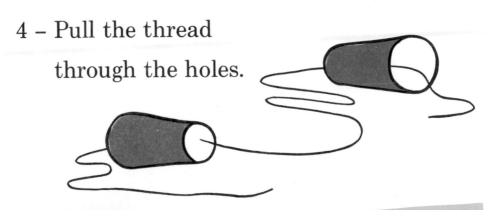

5 – Put some stickum
on the thread.
Stick the ends
inside the cups.

6 – Pull the thread tight
and talk into your cup.

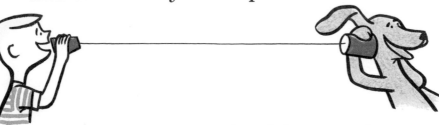

You can even talk with your dog
. . . if he knows how to talk.

How to Make
a
Stickit Picture

1 - Get some cardboard,
scissors, and a
lot of colored paper.

2 - Cut the paper into
a zillion pieces.

3 – Stick the pieces
on the cardboard.
Have fun! Stick them
any way you want to.

4 – Stick and stick,
and stick and stick!

When it's done
your mother will
hang it in your room.

Now make one for Mother.

How to Make
a
Creepy Willy

1 – Get some paper.

Get your scissors.

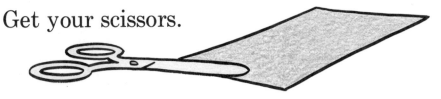

2 – Cut out a piece

of paper this big.

Draw his face on it.

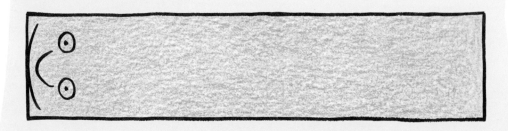

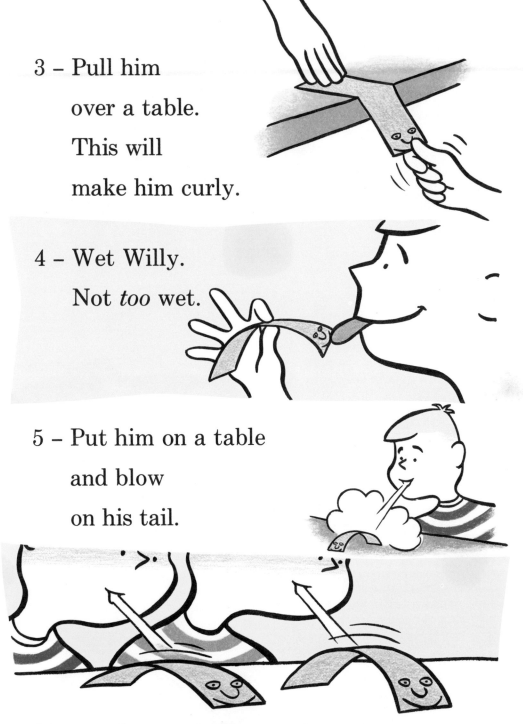

3 – Pull him over a table. This will make him curly.

4 – Wet Willy. Not *too* wet.

5 – Put him on a table and blow on his tail.

Have a Creepy Willy race!

How to Make

a

Nip Bug

1 – Get a clothespin.
   Get your scissors,
   some colored paper,
   glue and two tacks.

2 – Push the tacks
   in the clothespin.
   They are his eyes.

3 – Cut out some
paper legs and
glue them on.

4 – Cut out some wings.
Cut out a tail.
Color them
with funny dots.

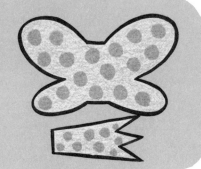

5 – Glue on his wings
and tail like this.

6 – Open the Nip Bug's
nipper . . .

. . . and nip him on anywhere.

How to Make

a

Huffel Hat

1 – Get a paper cup,
a string and
some straws.

2 – Put the straws on
the string like this.

36

3 – Tie the string
     around the straws.

4 – Make a hole
     in the top
     of the cup.

5 – Pull the string
     through the hole.

6 – Tie the string
     under your chin.

Your dog will think you are very pretty.

How to Make

a

Walking Thing

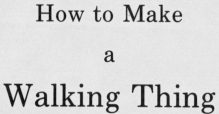

1 – Get a rubber band.
Get a spool and
two toothpicks.

2 – Rub some soap
on the spool.
Rub it on both ends.

3 – Put the rubber band
through the hole.

4 – Put the toothpicks
in the rubber band.

5 – Now wind up your
Walking Thing, and . . .

6 – Let it go for a walk!

How to Make

a

Clompy Clown

1 – Get a pair of scissors,
some stiff paper,
and some crayons.

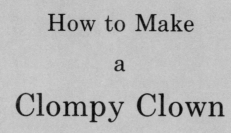

2 – Draw a clown
and cut him out.

3 – Stick one piece
in a ring like this.

4 – Put another piece
in the ring like this.

5 – Then stick that
one together.

6 – Stick another and another
and another and another.

Maybe you can make
a chain half a mile long!

How to Make

a

Spud Bunny

1 – You need a potato.
Toothpicks. Glue. Paper.
Scissors. Paper cup.
Three thumbtacks.

2 – Cut two big feet.
Cut two big ears.
Glue a toothpick
onto each ear.

3 – Stick a toothpick
into the potato.

4 – Push this toothpick
into the cup.
Glue the feet
on the cup.

5 – Push toothpicks
in for whiskers.

6 – Push the tacks in
for eyes and nose.
Push in the ears.

Now make the Spud Bunny's sister.

How to Grow

a

Goofy Garden

1 – Get a deep dish

and some

pretty little stones.

2 – Now get two carrots.
Eat them.
But save the tops.

3 – Put the stones
in the dish.
Pour some water
on the stones.

4 – Cut the carrot
tops like this.
Then put them
on the stones.

5 – Keep those stones wet.

Watch your
Goofy Garden grow.

How to Make
a
Tippy Top

1 – Get a piece of paper,
   a glass and a pencil.
   Scissors. Crayon.
   Also a toothpick.

2 – Put the glass
   on the paper.
   Draw around it
   with the pencil.

3 – Now cut out the
circle you made.
Draw this on it.

4 – Push the toothpick
through the center
of the paper.

5 – Give it a spin!
Spin it on a table.

How to Make

a

Parachute

1 – Ask your mother
for a paper napkin,
some thread, and
a clothespin.

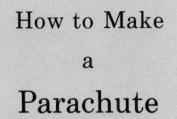

2 – Cut four pieces
of thread,
all two feet long.

3 – Tie the thread
   to the corners
   of the napkin.

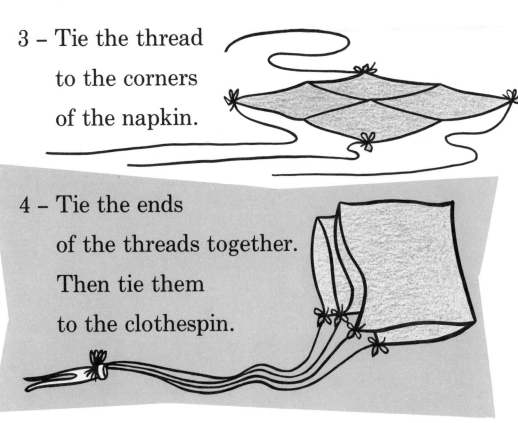

4 – Tie the ends
   of the threads together.
   Then tie them
   to the clothespin.

5 – Lay it all out
   very straight
   and roll it up.

Throw it as high
as you can.
But not in the house!

How to Make

a

Two-horned Noser

1 – Get a small paper bag,
crayons and scissors.

2 – Draw a face on the bag.
Make it a funny face.

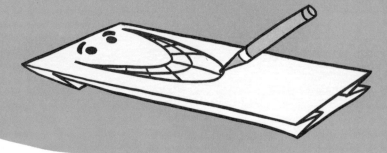

3 – Cut two holes in
   the top of the bag,
   and one where the
   nose goes.

4 – Put your hand
   in the bag.
   Put one finger
   in each hole.

5 – Now wiggle your horns
   and waggle your nose.

How to Make a
Wind Thing

1 – Get four paper cups,
   a piece of cardboard,
   some stickum, a bead,
   a pin, and a stick.

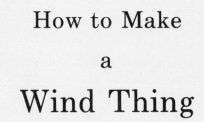

2 – Draw two lines
   on the cardboard
   like this.

3 – Now stick a cup
on each corner
with stickum.

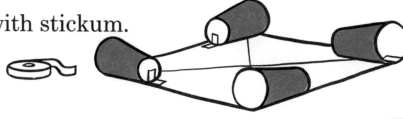

4 – Put the pin in
the cardboard
where the two
lines cross.

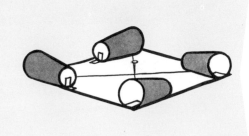

5 – Put the pin
through the bead.
Tap the pin
into the stick.

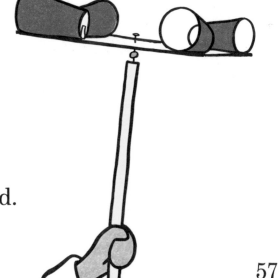

Now take it outside
and look for some wind.

How to Make
Birds Happy

1 – Get a milk box,
   scissors and
   some string.

2 – Ask your dad
   to cut the box
   like this.

3 – Have him make
    a hole here.

4 – Put the string
    through the hole.

5 – Put little pieces of bread
    in the bottom of the box.

6 – Hang it up
    in a tree.

Now your birds
will have a lunchroom!

How to Make

a

Moogle Mask

1 – You need a paper bag.

The biggest bag you can get.

2 – Draw a funny face
on the bag.
Cut two holes
for the eyes.

3 – Stick a paper cup
on for a nose.

4 – Cut out some hair.

   Stick it on.

5 – Cut out some glasses.

   Stick them on.

6 – Now put on your mask.

   None of your friends

   will know who you are!

ROBERT LOPSHIRE pre-tested everything in this book ... to make certain that your child would not get buried under a mountain of newspaper, string, tape, and glue. (Which is exactly what happened to *him* when he tried to make a *Snixitt*. The *Snixitt* is NOT included in this book.)

Mr. Lopshire attended two art schools in Boston, and has had a great variety of experience. As an artist he has done everything from advertising and fine art to industrial illustration.

He is also famous for another Beginner Book—PUT ME IN THE ZOO—a happy piece of nonsense that delights children again and again. The source of its inspiration was Robert Lopshire's birthplace, Sarasota, Florida, the winter home of the circus.

3 – Now color him.

Make him funny!

4 – Cut out two holes

for his legs.

5 – He can run!

He can dance!

Why not make two of them?

How to Make
Ding Dong Music

1 – Ask your mother
   for four old
   glasses and a
   wooden spoon.

2 – Put this much water
   in one glass.

3 – Put this much
   in another glass.

4 – Put this much
in the next glass.

5 – Put this much
in the last one.

6 – Stand the glasses
in front of you
like this.

7 – Tap them.
Don't hit them
too hard.

Play along with the music
from your radio or TV.

How to Make

a

Link Link Chain

1 – Get some paper,
   some scissors,
   and some glue.

2 – Cut the paper
   in strips like this.